A STATISTICAL STUDY OF RANDOMNESS

poems by

Kendra Nuttall

Finishing Line Press
Georgetown, Kentucky

A STATISTICAL STUDY
OF RANDOMNESS

Copyright © 2021 by Kendra Nuttall
ISBN 978-1-64662-463-8 First Edition
All rights reserved under International and Pan-American Copyright Conventions.
No part of this book may be reproduced in any manner whatsoever without written
permission from the publisher, except in the case of brief quotations embodied in
critical articles and reviews.

ACKNOWLEDGMENTS

Thank you to the editors of the following journals in which several of these
poems, or earlier versions, first appeared:

Across the Social Distances (2020): "I Miss Nickel Arcades."
Califragile (2020): "It's the Little Things."
Capsule Stories (Isolation Edition 2020): "Aftershock."
Capsule Stories (Summer 2020): "The Widow."
Chiron Review (Fall 2020): "Sedentary."
Emotional Alchemy: Tales From the Front Porch (2020): "Portrait of a Small
        Town: Before", "Portrait of a Small Town: After."
Fearsome Critters: A Journal of Millennial Art (Volume 1, 2018): "Lo Siento."
Maudlin House (2017): "Isn't It Nice."
Poetry in the Time of Coronavirus (Volume 2, 2020): "Fragile"
Spectrum Literary Journal (2020): "On Dropped Eggs and Spilled Milk, or
        Why I'm Never Having Children."
Touchstones (Spring 2018): "America the Beautiful"; "A Statistical Study of
        Randomness" (First Place Poetry Winner); "Willie."
What Rough Beast (2019): "There Is No Playground Along the U.S.-Mexico
        Border."

Publisher: Leah Huete de Maines
Editor: Christen Kincaid
Cover Art and Design: Lori Tsou
Author Photo: Kenzie Klumker of KZ Studios Photography

Order online: www.finishinglinepress.com
            also available on amazon.com

Author inquiries and mail orders:
Finishing Line Press
P. O. Box 1626
Georgetown, Kentucky 40324
U. S. A.

Table of Contents

Part Four

Part Five

To Mom and Dad.
Thank you for everything.

PART ONE

The Greenland shark can live up to 500 years.

A STATISTICAL STUDY OF RANDOMNESS

Physical pain or emotional pain?   11% of Americans suffer from chronic pain.

Pepsi or coke?   Let me take your pain away.

Luz got married to keep her husband in the country; he's a Dreamer. They'll never

get the wedding Luz dreamed of.

Keep dreaming.   Pessimist or optimist?

Summer or winter?   50% of marriages end in divorce.   I promise, not mine.

Who's next?   40% of people are unhappy in their marriages.

I promise, I won't be.

Confession: I look at wedding dresses online every day.

Sweet or savory?

I lost thirty pounds when I was depressed.   Jealous?

5% of the world's population is depressed.   Hugs or kisses?

Writers are more prone to depression than the general population.

Everyone counts   calories   sometimes I think.

8 million people in the U.S. have an eating disorder.

Ice cream or frozen yogurt?

I gained two pounds this week.

I don't care   too much.

Early bird or night owl?

Confession: I used to cry in the bathroom every day, now I cry in bed at night—

only some nights.

Grandpa fell in the bathroom at the fair.   Is it fair?   Spring or fall?

1.3 million elderly Americans live in nursing homes.

Grandma doesn't want to go.

Am I happy?   I am loved.

Cats or dogs? My cat died; 1.5 million shelter animals are euthanized every year.

My dad has cancer.   1 in 8 women will get breast cancer.

Grandpa died.

He was loved.   He is loved.

The average casket costs about $2000.   My college tuition costs about $2000.

Video games or board games?

34,000 people commit suicide each year.

Who's next?

Chocolate or vanilla?   39% of people worldwide are overweight.

Fries or kale?

Thanksgiving or Christmas?

There are 4.6 million mentally disabled adults in the U.S.

They are often forgotten,   invisible.
Amber used to be homeless.

There are over 500,000 homeless people in America.

House or apartment?

Amber hasn't seen her family since last Christmas.

I gave you my heart.

I cried every day in December.

Books or movies?

480,000 people die from smoking each year.   Sparkling water or regular water?

The person you love is 73% water.

480,000 deaths could be prevented.

But we'll spend 168 billion dollars a year to help them.   Death or taxes?

86 people die per day from gun violence.

Who's next?   God or no God?

The annual cost of gun violence in the U.S. is 229 billion dollars.

Money or love?

Burial or cremation?   Too much?

46% of Americans have a loved one who is addicted to drugs.

Comedy or tragedy?

Is crying as healthy as laughter?   A baby is born every 8 seconds.
     Someone dies every 11 seconds.   Who's next?

Am I happy?

I am   I think.

Eyes or lips?   30,000 people fall in love every day.

Why is love hard?

Flowers or chocolate?

Confession: I almost bought the engagement ring I wanted.

I'm crazy   but just a little bit

right?   Keep dreaming.   Whitney got divorced when she was 20.

Breakfast or dinner?

I care   too much.

I'm afraid of death.   100% of people die.

Why am I afraid?

100% of people are afraid of something.

Am I happy?

I'm okay.

Right hand or left hand?

Hot or cold?   Marvel or DC?

Hello or goodbye?

Star Wars or Star Trek?   Is this over yet?   Quit complaining.

PORTRAIT OF A SMALL TOWN: BEFORE

The honeymooners are home
from war. Grandma and Grandpa

are young and in love. New roses
bloom and mothers hold children's

hands as they cross the street to greet
the mailman, the milkman, and

the middle school teacher. Rumor
is she's *expecting*. Elmo's store is open,

best candy in Bingham County. Kids
run barefoot across pavement chasing

dogs and peacocks. Potato fields flourish.
The women make funeral potatoes and

green jello for the neighborhood party.
The church choir is practicing for Easter.

Grandma sits on the shore of the Snake
River sunbathing as her kids skip rocks.

Grandpa puts the finishing touches on
the family home. My father picks a flower

and tucks it behind his mother's ear before
flying off to answer the call of a distant voice.

IN WHICH I CONTEMPLATE MORTALITY WHILE CUDDLING MY DOG

She will be middle-aged
at six years old and

that is life's greatest sadness.
Time ticking on and ticking off

without a care.

PLEASANT GROVE, UTAH

Yesterday, it was called
Battle Creek. Dollhouses are
          covered in ivy walls

and red bricks. White picket
fences dot rose bed and bird bath
          bespeckled yards.

There's a dog, usually
a goldendoodle or a lab,
          lapping up sprinkler water

as kids screech and cry like kids do.
Mothers scoop them up and
          bandage their budding egos.

                    *

Yesterday, the Utes were a tribe,
picketed in deserts, washed away
          by the Mormon militia.

The Utes didn't steal Brigham's horses,
only lived in the mountains
          we call home,

but that was enough. Sometime later
someone put a plaque where
          the battle happened.

It doesn't say who died. Hikers go
up the mountain to take Instagram
          photos.

MY NEIGHBOR THE HOARDER

She is queen of the junkyard, lover of maltese poodle mixes, Walmart Liz Taylor decked in discount department store dresses, plastic pearls, and pin-up girl polka dots. She sinks into mid-century forest sofas, Edwardian chaises, and patio picnic tables. She recedes into sunflower yellow wallpaper, pepto-bismol pink paint, and smoke-stained white walls.

　　　　She's not a smoker, but 　　fireplace ash and dog vomit soaks into her carrot carpet. She's taller than her hunchbacked husband, whose unsteady hands vaccinate puppies and calves.

　　　　He's ninety-something, doesn't know who I am. 　　　　　　　　His wife comes home with a new dog, a new dress, a used set of golf clubs for the great-grandkid's first birthday.

　　　　It's a good idea. 　　She shows me her wedding photo with the first husband. They were the same height. He died in Vietnam. The second husband died of old age. She looked pretty with her teal eyeshadow and box-dyed platinum blonde hair. The black and white TV plays static. The color TV plays *Lawrence Welk*. The radio plays Rush Limbaugh. 　　　　　Another, Elvis. 　　　　　　　She dances as she cleans the dog vomit. 　　　　Dead roses fill three vases. Dried daffodils hang next to bible verses and glued-together cat puzzles. She remembers Disneyland's opening day. 　　　　　She stoops to feed the dogs M&Ms.

　　　　She remembers the tiffany-blue Cadillac, 　　　　was always jealous of the neighbor with Tiffany jewelry. 　　　　　Always jealous of the housewife who could bake. 　　　Always wanted the world, 　　　bought as much as she could.

WILLIE

Past the automatic doors
that aren't so automatic
and the cashier with cigarette skin and
communist-red fingernails,

past the toddler screaming for candy
and the teenager checking out long legs
in short shorts—all wide-eyed and gawky,

past the spilled salsa in aisle seven,
in the middle of Saturday rush, you'll see him.
Black apron, blond mustache bouncing over
a wrinkled mouth shouting out to the crowd. If you let him,

he'll tell you about summers spent in Santa Barbara, about
owning a restaurant and bar, about
leaving because California was too loud, about
his son having the cutest baby ever, about
his Mormon wife rounding out his lapsed Episcopalian, about
getting his first wife pregnant at 17, about
marrying her because that's what good people do, about
his first divorce (and second and third), about
how women used to put effort into their appearance, about
how men used to have the balls to marry a woman, about
how men used to be strong (none of this cry-baby crap), about
the horrendous traffic on State Street, about
the orchard he owns on 700 North, about
how this valley used to be just orchards, about
how this valley used to be so quiet, and now
it's getting so loud,

all while he hands you a sample of microwaved
quiche. You can find it in the freezer section
on sale today for $2.99.
Thank you for shopping at WinCo.

FAMILY SPECIAL

My dad digs through mail
for restaurant coupons.
Taco Tuesday, two-for-ones,
          family specials.

Let's go. We drive past
my community college
and he asks me how I'm doing.
We buy a bundle of tacos and
beefy cheesy burritos and eat
until the bloat hurts
in a sticky boogery booth.
I should ask how he's doing, but
I don't want to cry about cancer
at Taco Bell,

because that's just too easy
in this throw-up pink postmodern pastel
rainbow relic from hell.
So, we talk about video games
and how to do taxes
          and forget.

Or maybe it was Del Taco.

WINTER SPRING

It is the day after my father's death
and spring blooms in our living room.

A bouquet of yellow roses brighter
than Christmas tree lights, white

lilies next to the Nativity set,
a blanket of forget-me-nots over

baby Jesus, chrysanthemums
sitting on Santa's lap—all turning

my mother's mourning into dancing
as she remembers the songs my father

played. He never made it to radio,
but he's famous in this house just

the same. He didn't ask for flowers,
but family, friends, neighbors I never

met—everyone remembers him.
Three days after Christmas, stuck

on snowed-in streets, sipping hot
chocolate, and snuggling with

the ones they love, they're thinking
about him—they're thinking about us.

ONE MAN BAND DINER

We spent spring break at
        Zion.
I didn't like camping.
I don't think Dad did either.
His knees were too old to kneel
next to campfires, but he was at that
        middle age
where men try to recapture youth. I hiked
        Angel's Landing
with a blister on my foot and granola in hand.
Dad huffed and puffed his way up to the top. We didn't
        sleep well,
so, to home it was. We drove past red rocks,
        ghost towns,
and green hills. You used to
be able to see One Man Band Diner from the
        freeway,
before Lehi was called Silicon Slopes. Even then,
One Man Band was a place frozen
        in time.
The jukebox played Elvis and the silver-haired patrons
swooned. You had to pick up a corded red telephone
to place an order. I hadn't seen a corded telephone
        in years.
We ate Navajo tacos. I picked off the onions and iceberg
lettuce. Dad ate my onions and iceberg lettuce and we talked.
About math homework, about piano lessons, about our
        next adventure.
I ate at One Man Band again this week. The Navajo taco
tasted just as I remembered. The music and faces were
just as old. Dad's funeral was two
        years ago.

PORTRAIT OF A SMALL TOWN: AFTER

Peacocks flaunt their feathers on
top of junkyards and forgotten weeds, kings

of the ghost town. My father is buried there,
near his childhood home. His childhood friends

came to his funeral. I wonder what that's like,
to have lifelong friends. To know everyone's

name. To know each peacock and alpaca,
each dog and Doris and Bob. We used to

get slushies from Elmo's store—VHS tapes
and cassettes for half off, dusty cigarettes

behind the counter—a dusty cigarette of
a town. Potato fields and potato smells

for miles around. We used to skip rocks
in the Snake River. We used to take walks

on the shore. We used to have family
reunions, until the grandkids grew up and

Grandpa grew old. He's buried next to
my father. That's the only reason anyone

goes now, to put flowers on their graves
and watch as the Idaho wind carries them away.

PART TWO

**1 in 4 Americans speak a second language.
I haven't opened Duolingo in a month.**

TALKING

I can't get into podcasts—I'm not into talking.
Why do you think I'm a writer?
I thought radio already did the whole talking thing anyway.
Rush Limbaugh screeching, my dad agreeing.
Conspiracy theories, religious theory—
radio raised a generation of anti-everything.
The day-time shows for stay-at-homes—
they did the talking thing too.
Dr. Oz and Dr. Phil and The Doctors and Oprah
interviewing doctors—dishing out medical advice
in the same sentence as essential oil. You get a snake oil,
and you get a snake oil—everyone gets a snake oil!
And the nightly news, talking about serial killers
and car wrecks and death. How handsome Ted Bundy was —
did you know he lived in Utah? He was Mormon too.
I said my first word at nine months, according to my mom.
In Kindergarten, the kids thought I couldn't talk.
The only feedback at parent-teacher conference was,
"Good student, wish she would talk more."
I've never learned how.
How to stand in front of a classroom of teenagers and say,
"Hey, the Oxford comma is pretty cool."
How to ask a stranger, "Would you please
take my photo so I have a tangible memory
of this once-in-a-lifetime vacation?"
How to talk on the phone, how to order food,
how to tell the waiter to stop filling my water glass—
seriously, why? The glass is half full.
How to, how to. I can't get into podcasts because it's just
talking, talking, talking. Let's get back into reading—
good-old-fashioned books of talking
in our hands and thoughts best left in the head.

VIVIR MI VIDA

My mother never learned
how to ride a bike or how to swim.
She never learned all the lyrics to a song,
just *vivir mi vida, la la la la* on repeat, but
she learned two languages.

First: English.
I before E except after
esposo and *dios* and *hija*.

A pronoun: *I*
    A verb: *I miss*
        A noun: *I miss Venezuela.*

Second: Love.
Womb and tomb are not pronounced
the way they're spelled. A womb is life.
A tomb is death. Love doesn't end.

Te quiero.
    Te extraño.
        One question:
Why?
There are too many ways to say I miss you.
There are not enough ways to say I love you.
There are too many years and at the same time

there will never be enough,

    just
        vivir mi vida.
          Live my life.

THE TOWER OF BABEL

My great-aunt is almost one hundred years old.
We've never spoken. I don't speak my mother

tongue. Genesis says we speak different languages
because we built The Tower of Babel to make a name

for ourselves. God, ever-loving and egotistical
as he is, decided it was his name or the highway, so

he cursed us with babble and spread us around like
peanut butter and jelly across the sandwich of the planet

to start our own tongues. Make a name for yourself
now. My mother's ancestors came from Spain and

Senegal. She's a descendant of conquistadors and slaves.
My father's ancestors came from England and Germany.

He's a descendant of Mormon pioneers. I come from two
worlds. I live in one. I don't speak my mother tongue.

THE WIDOW

My mother blossomed
after my father's death.

Don't get me wrong,
she was always a spider killer and

a mean pastelito maker, but
somewhere between the funeral potatoes

and the daily diet Coke,
God spoke:

You don't have to
cook dinner for a man every day.

Don't sit in the cancer
hospital waiting for words

that will never come.
Don't hold a cold hand

when you could hold
me. Please.

She believed in God.
I believed in her

and pastelitos with cheese
on the backyard swing.

She got a full-time job
with insurance and time off

and a brand-new bedroom
where the sun shines on yellow.

She dances with neighbors
to department store sales

and dances alone
to La Bamba,

but it's not sad anymore.
Por ti seré, for you I'll be.

It was the only song
my father sang.

My mother sings to me.
For you I'll be.

LO SIENTO

¿Cómo estás?
I'm not a Dreamer, but I don't look so different. I'm lucky.

¿Hablas español?
It's my own fault I don't.

¿Qué tiempo hace?
It's still winter here. Most of the people blend in with the snow.

¿Cuántos años tienes?
When I was three, I spoke Spanish. At school, the kids spoke English; I didn't want to embarrass myself.

¿Cuántos años tienes?
Too old for excuses.

¿De dónde eres?
I'm from Idaho, my mom is Venezuelan.

¿Quién eres tú?
Mom wanted to name me Alejandra. Dad said no one could spell it. I'm Kendra.

¿De dónde es tu familia?
Venezuela is far away. I visited once when I was little; I don't remember it. I don't remember my family.

¿De dónde es tu familia?
My cousin, Cesandry, is beautiful. Her family fled to Brazil.

¿De dónde eres?
I'm just a little tan. Mom can't hide her accent.

¿Dónde vives?
White people say racist things to Mom on the phone. This is where we live.

¿Quién eres tú?
People think I'm Mexican, but they aren't mean to me. My skin is lighter than the others.

¿Cuál es tu lugar favorito?
Mom used to say she wanted to go back to Venezuela. Now it's impossible. My favorite place is bed.

¿Cuál es tu color favorito?
Abuelita's favorite perfume is Japanese cherry blossom. Pink reminds me of her.

¿A dónde vas?
I haven't seen my abuelita in five years. She made the best pastelitos. We've never had a conversation.

¿Hablas español?
I'm sorry I didn't try in eighth grade Spanish class.

¿Tienes remordimientos?

I'm afraid I'll never see my abuelita again. I'm afraid I'll lose her before I ever learn to speak.

¿Estás bien?

I'm Venezuelan. Venezuela is dying. I'm sorry I don't speak Spanish.

¿Quién eres tú?

I'm Venezuelan. I dream.

PART THREE

Bald eagles have a wingspan of 7 feet.

THERE IS NO PLAYGROUND ALONG
THE U.S.-MEXICO BORDER

Yesterday, Johan took his first steps;
today he wears dress shoes and a diaper to court.
He doesn't know that American Dream—
the one with purple mountain majesties,
amber waves of grain, and white picket fences.

Pursuing happiness,
someone built a seesaw at the Southern border.
Through slats in a wall over an invisible line,
under one spacious sky,
kids got to do what kids do best:
play.

Johan doesn't know that American Dream—
the one with millionaires in McMansions
and migrants in McDonald's, low wages
from sea to plasticized sea, spray can cheese,
mass incarceration, mass deportation, huddled masses
yearning to breathe
free.

Johan's parents were deported to Honduras five months ago.
The judge asks Johan, "What do you want?"
He doesn't know how to talk,
but a seesaw would be a lot of fun.

PRIVILEGE

A butter knife is just a butter knife   until you look the opposite way
SPF 50 for your skin   to avoid peeling the wound
A BA isn't BS   because of student loans
An MFA isn't impossible   because you're broke
You care about these acronyms   because the American Dream means
Someone cares about you   always out of reach
Rent is due   like medical bills
It's not scary   like a butter knife.

TIME OFF

I got a new job
with 12 paid days off.

Four for New York;
the tickets were cheap.

One for the cold
I'll get from a co-worker.

Two for the flu, 'cause
of the co-worker again.

Three for the Catalina cruise
and bottomless booze.

One to visit my mother,
she hasn't seen me in a while.

One to visit the doctor,
he hasn't seen me in a while.

One for a job interview—
wait, never mind.

AMERICA THE BEAUTIFUL

Dayton, Ohio, August 4, 2019:
We laughed and drank to life.
El Paso, Texas, August 3, 2019:
We shopped for groceries and back-to-school supplies.
Virginia Beach, Virginia, May 31, 2019:
We were getting ready to go home after work.
Thousand Oaks, California, November 7, 2018:
We stomped our feet to Brooks & Dunn.
Pittsburgh, Pennsylvania, October 27, 2018:
We prayed under the Tree of Life.
Santa Fe, Texas, May 18, 2018:
We went to school.
Parkland, Florida, February 14, 2018:
We went to school.
Sutherland Springs, Texas, November 5, 2017:
We worshipped and praised God on Sunday morning.
Las Vegas, Nevada, October 1, 2017:
We danced to country music under the setting sun.
Orlando, Florida, June 12, 2016:
We felt safe feeling the pulse of music, the pulse of hearts.
San Bernardino, California, December 2, 2015:
We celebrated Christmas reluctantly together as coworkers.
Roseburg, Oregon, October 1, 2015:
We went to school.
Aurora, Colorado, July 20, 2012:
We attended a midnight movie premiere.
Newtown, Connecticut, December 14, 2012:
We went to school.
Fort Hood, Texas, November 5, 2009:
We fought and lived to protect our country from terrorism.
Blacksburg, Virginia, April 16, 2007:
We went to school.
Columbine, Colorado, April 20, 1999:
We went to school.
Killeen, Texas, October 16, 1991:
We ordered soups and sandwiches for lunch.
San Ysidro, California, July 19, 1984:

We ate happy meals under the ketchup-stained arches.
Austin, Texas, August 1, 1966:
We went to school.

SEDENTARY

It's not the industrial age
anymore but we like tradition

too much—pledging allegiance,
apple pie, hard labor—

America. We commute
ourselves to office chairs, glue

our eyes to blue light screens,
hold our breath and count to 8.

We wear our back pain to bed,
wake up, and do it again

while the kids grow up on diet Coke
and balloon like mortgages.

Our pants are adjusted for inflation,
our salaries are sedentary,

and we're doing just fine
hanging on by a single bootstrap.

SPRING AT THE CEMETERY

Look at them fluttering from grave to grave,
only moments from cradle, chasing a butterfly.

They trip over a patchworked quilt of uneven
grass, different shades of green gleaming

in the after-rain. A toddler cries. A mother rises
from her knees, turning away from cold stone

to warm hand. *It's okay, it's okay.* Yellow
and blue butterflies float among the Memorial

Day flowers, landing just for a second before
the children chase them away. *It's okay, it's okay.*

PART FOUR

Pet owners are happier than petless people.
"Petless" is a made-up word.

AFTERSHOCK

Waking up to an earthquake
is the last thing I'd expect,
but, here I am, sitting in pajamas
I've worn four days in a row
wondering if I'm dreaming,
wondering if I'm somehow on my cancelled European cruise,
wondering if the Book of Revelation and R.E.M are actually right.

It's half past seven.
The memes have been made.
The news articles have been posted.
The aftershocks will continue.

I haven't left my apartment
since Saturday afternoon after I stocked up
on a supply of glittery sanitizer
from my diabetic mother.
I think about

my mother going to work
at the health department call center.
They won't let her stay home.
I think about

my husband,
donating blood amid the chaos
of grocery hoarders, price gougers,
and apathetic spring breakers.
I think about

my brother-in-law's brewery
shutting down;
                    how small we really are.
I think about

my father,
as I often do. Maybe he was lucky cancer

killed him before the virus. At least then I could
say goodbye. Today, I can't enter a hospital room.
I think about

hospital rooms, the smells of bleach
and Lysol, the sounds of ventilators and sighs
and   silence.
I look at

my dog sprawled across the bed,
sound asleep, totally, blissfully
unaware
of the aftershock to come.

THIS IS NOT AN AD FOR CHAPSTICK

Pick and repeat. Smear Chapstick across
my chapped lips. Pick and repeat. Teens

always talk back. Remember before
they knew what unconditional love meant,

but lived it? My husband likes coffee, just six
mugs a day. And open cupboards. And spit

splashed on the bathroom mirror. Rinse and
repeat. There are only so many times one can

watch *Titanic* before it's pathetic. Only so many
pizza slices one can stuff before the gut rebels.

Chapstick makes everything feel better. Pick and
repeat. Skin flakes look like snowflakes. Pick and

repeat. I like contactless delivery because it means
I don't have to talk to you. I like working from home

because it means I don't have to talk to you.
My lips are too chapped to move. Pick and repeat.

IT'S THE LITTLE THINGS

like lavender and lemon drifting
through the air from the essential oil factory,

sunlight coming through the windows,
and my dog snoring in bed.

Like kolaches fresh out of the oven,
cookies on my doorstep, and

my husband playing the same song
on the guitar over and over,

until I imagine myself somewhere
in the Caribbean, before cruise ships

became Titanic and *Titanic* was just a movie.
When a titanic disaster wasn't just an iceberg

or a cough away. It's the little things like talking
on the phone with my mother and writing poetry about

old shipwrecks and new pandemics to pass the time
until words and pictures on screens become reality.

I MISS NICKEL ARCADES

       The coppery smell of coins,
the stench of pubescent teens,
dirty diapers.

A disgusting, delightful mess
       of casino sounds and pizza
guts coating the floor.

       And the games,
the button-mashing,
screen-swiping
sweat-inducing games.

A germophobe's worst nightmare,
       a pandemic's home.
The nickel arcade is closed.

       I don't know
if it will ever open again.
Admission for a nickel is great
on a good day.

FRAGILE

I miss the mall.
Hard pretzels and 90s carpet,
stores with stupid names
like DressBarn and Hot Dog on a Stick.

The peach fuzz on my upper lip isn't
so peachy and the 11s
between my eyes are turning into 12s.

I'm too old for TikTok.
In one year, you'll be too young.

I want to be like Jane Fonda
someday.
But even Jane Fonda feels time.

        We're fragile

like guinea pigs,
like made-in-China plates,
like high school sweetheart marriages

ending before we have a chance
          to begin.

What will high school history textbooks
say thirty years from now
when schools have budgets
for new books?

The economy doesn't know
there's more than one kind
of great depression.

WATER BEAR

The tardigrade is in retrograde, still
in yesterday's vacuum as earth spins
forward and the aspiring ballet dancer

falls—
       my first heartbreak. I never
learned to dance. I never learned
to swim. I never practiced piano,
just listened to Clair de Lune setting
the birds in the trees dreaming
as the fountains sobbed.

The waterfall lifts her bridal veil
to watch her father disappear—

       the hardest of heartbreaks.
Where is the tardigrade, little water bear?
I hope he's swimming somewhere on the moon
before childhood's impending doom.

ISN'T IT NICE

when middle aged ladies at your mom's
birthday party
in Olive Garden compliment the black dress
you bought yesterday
and tell you you're getting too skinny
for your own good
but they wish they had that problem
and *you're so beautiful*
please stop growing up I remember
when you were young.
There's nothing you can do about
getting old.
That dress won't fit forever and that
face will change and
you'll sit in an Olive Garden seeing
some other girl
and wouldn't it be nice if things could
always be the same.

PART FIVE

This book is not a statistical study of randomness.

WHEN THE COMPUTER BREAKS

I miss my dad most when the computer breaks.
The repair guy doesn't understand what's wrong.

It's broken like my mom's heart, I say. Understand?
No? Ok. The screen faded to black, like Uncle Ben,

David Bowie, my childhood cat. It let go, like Rose.
Kaput like the Death Star. Sodom and Gomorrah.

Game of Thrones Season Eight. Understand? No?
Ok. The task manager quit due to poor working

conditions, like I quit my job at the call center after
two weeks. Like you're going to quit this job. The mouse

starved to death because there's no cheese. The monitor
is unmonitored, like Mormons on their honeymoon.

Understand? No? Ok. When the computer breaks, I miss
my dad. Can you fix that? Can computers resurrect yet?

I'M TIRED OF FINGERNAILS

growing too fast
like Instagram baby
moneymakers.
It's not fair
that fingernails grow
while hot royal husbands
go bald. And for what?
So I can paint my nails
like the Sistine ceiling,
without any of Michelangelo's
artistry? I can't even
stay in the lines. And if I cut
too close to the nailbed,
it feels like lying on a bed of nails.
If I let them grow, every bathroom
trip is a biohazard. And if I somehow
manage to get the perfect length,
it only lasts for a day. I guess
that's just how good things go
until they don't.

ON DROPPED EGGS AND SPILLED MILK, OR WHY I'M NEVER HAVING CHILDREN

I become prisoner
      to the dairy aisle,
trapped between a shopping cart
      and an obese woman
yelling at Bertram to put the eggs down.
      Plop,
the eggs drop.
      Bertram laughs in the face
of wrath.
      That's what happens
when you name a kid Bertram.
      Excuse me,
I just need some milk
      but Bertram spills that too.

PRIMEVIL

This order is not eligible for two-day shipping
but I need it

like I need to baby-talk
kittens and guinea pigs.

Like I need to scratch a good boy
behind the ears.

Like I need to pick my lips
while watching TV.

Like I need to pick onions
out of everything.

Like I need to caress the stubble
on my legs.

Like I need to caress the stubble
on your chest.

Like,
I really need it.

VASOVAGAL SYNCOPE

It's not a dirty phrase; it rhymes with
      bagel and killer bee.
There's nothing dirty about vaginas anyway. Don't
      tell me that's not the first
word that comes to mind. Vasobagel Killerbee starts with
      the horror of the glaucoma
puff experienced one too many times. That's what I get for
      sensitive eyes and thicc glasses.
I bring all the boys to the exam. I bring you to watch me
      faint as the optometrist
pries open my lids like a gynecologist pries open legs
      looking for disease.
My eyeballs are footballs and my cervix is a donut.
      The latter is normal,
the first is not. I'm pale, clammy, nauseous, and totally not
      describing clam chowder.
I'm seeing stars or maybe it's the letter E splattered
      across the universe
on the poster in front of me. I might die, but thanks
      for holding my hand
as the Shopko lights flicker and the optometrist
      hands me tap water
while I heave over the trash can looking at soggy
      contacts and eye
cancer pamphlets. *This happens all the time*
      doesn't cheer me up.
Take 10% off frames won't cut it. Shopko can shove it.
      See you next year.

FEEDING THE MULTITUDE

The veins on the back of my hand are shaped like the ichthys,
Jesus fish. It is said that Jesus fed five thousand with five loaves

and two fishes. I would like to believe in miracles, but Facebook
makes it difficult. What would Facebook commenters say of Jesus'

miracle? Fake news. I could feed ten thousand. Was the bread
gluten-free? It's no wonder Christ hasn't come back. I've considered

getting my hand tattooed, just for fun. Turn my Jesus fish into
a goldfish with little googly eyes. It would be a miracle if social media

said nothing, but I suppose we're all socially distanced strangers
shouting into the void—hungry for the Second Coming, or something.

A STATISTICAL STUDY OF RANDOMNESS: VOLUME II

Truth or lies?

I got married.   Ball gown or mermaid dress?

       The average American wedding costs $35,329.

Mine was $2,000.

                                                       I was happy.

                             Dad died.

       He walked me down the aisle.

              The wedding photographer lost all the ceremony photos.

The average wedding photographer costs $2,814.   Mine was $400.

       I wrote my dad's obituary.   Books or ebooks?

   I spoke at his funeral.

                     The average funerals costs $7,000.

I miss him.   I love him.   I love you.

What's next?

                             I got a job.

              99% of people lose money in multi-level marketing.

   I left the job.

              The current unemployment rate in the U.S. is 14.7%.

I feel bad.

I'm having a quarter-life crisis.

What's next?

I went to Cambodia to teach English.

Holiday in Cambodia or Party in the USA?

David went to the hospital.

1 in 13 people have asthma.   David almost died in Cambodia.

The hospital bill was $1,200.

Can't complain.
60% of all bankruptcies in the U.S. are due to medical costs.

Our security guard in Cambodia was 12 years old and homeless.

We came home.   I didn't teach English in Cambodia.

It's a party in the USA.

Over three billion people live on less than $2.50 a day.

Can't complain.

Cruise in Europe or Alaska?

Unemployed.   The U.S. federal minimum wage is $7.25.

McDonald's or Burger King?

I'm gaining weight.
It's just aging.

100% of people age.

I don't want to.

Dad was 60 years old.   Mammogram or colonoscopy?

There was another shooting today.

                              What's next?

                                        200,000 acres of rainforest are burned a day.

5,892,560 tons of plastic waste are in the ocean.

                              Paper or plastic?

Blind or deaf?

                              The United States holds 4.4% of the world's population.

            There are 7,684,114,855 people in the world.

                                             Are they happy?

            The United States holds 22% of the world's prisoners.

                                             Rehab or reoffend?

            I was happy.

                              Are you happy?

            I know four people who have tried to kill themselves.

                                        I'm a realist.

                                        Sunshine or rainbows?

                              This is America.

This is the world.

            I care   too much.

44% of Americans own a dog.

           29% of Americans own a cat.

             2% of Americans own a guinea pig.

I like guinea pigs.

        Moon or stars?

                I haven't seen the stars in years.

    What's next?

                Maybe we'll go to Mars.

      100% of people dream.   Dreams or nightmares?

Can't complain.

      Everything will be okay.

              Okay.

Kendra Nuttall is a copywriter by day and poet by night. She earned her BA in English from Utah Valley University (UVU) in 2018. Kendra was a first-place poetry winner in UVU's *Touchstones* journal and a presenter and winner at UVU's 2019 Showcase Awards. Her work has appeared in *Spectrum, Capsule Stories, Chiron Review, Maudlin House,* and various other literary journals and anthologies. She lives in Utah with her husband and fellow writer, David Lindsay, and poodle, Belle. When she's not writing, you can find her hiking around Utah, watching reality TV, or attempting to pet every animal she sees. Find her online at kendranuttall.com.

www.ingramcontent.com/pod-product-compliance
Lightning Source LLC
Chambersburg PA
CBHW021202090426
42740CB00008B/1205